Christmas Themed JOKES

For Men

Copyright 2023

CONTENTS

Jokes	1
Knock-Knock Jokes	47
Funny Ideas	56
Tongue Twisters	63
Silly Stories	75
Riddles	83

JOKES

Ho, ho, ho, better put that hot chocolate down before these jokes make you spill your drink!

What do you get
if you cross
a snowman
and a vampire?

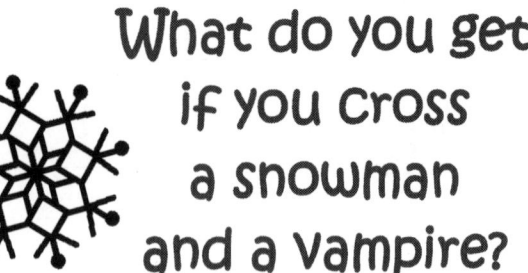

Frostbite!

What says Oh, Oh, Oh?

Santa walking backward!

Why was the snowman looking through the carrots?

He was picking his nose!

How does a snowman get around?

By riding an "icicle!"

Why did Santa's helper see the psychiatrist?

Because he had a low "elf" esteem!

Why did the Christmas tree go to the barber?

It needed a trim!

What do you call Santa when he gets stuck in the chimney?

Claus-trophobic!

What do you call Father Christmas on the beach?

Sandy Claus!

What do elves post on social media?

Elf-ies!

What do you call an obnoxious reindeer?

RUDE-olph!

What do snowmen eat for breakfast?

Ice Crispies!

What do Mexican sheep say at Christmas time?

Fleece Navidad!

What do you call
a cat on the
beach during
Christmas time?

Sandy Claws!

What do you
call a snowman
with a six-pack?

An abdominal snowman!

Why did the snowman win the Christmas talent show?

Because he was outstanding in his field!

What do you call Santa's little helpers?

Subordinate
Clauses!

What do you get when you cross a bell with a skunk?

Jingle Smells!

Why did the elf push his bed into the fireplace?

He wanted to sleep like a log!

What kind of music do elves love the most?

Wrap music!

Why did Santa's workshop get shut down by the health department?

For elf and safety reasons!

What do you call a bankrupt Santa?

Saint Nickel-less!

Why did the gingerbread man go to the doctor?

He felt crumby!

What do you call a snowman with a temper?

Melt-down!

Why did the elf go to school?

To learn his "elf"-abet!

How do Christmas trees access the internet?

They log in!

Why did the man put his wallet in the freezer?

He wanted cold hard cash for Christmas shopping!

Why did the man think the Christmas tree was knitting?

It kept dropping its needles!

What did the man say
when he bought
a pair of socks
for Christmas?

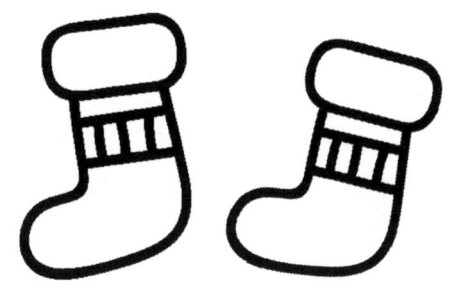

"These are stocking stuffer material!"

Why did the man sit on the Christmas lights?

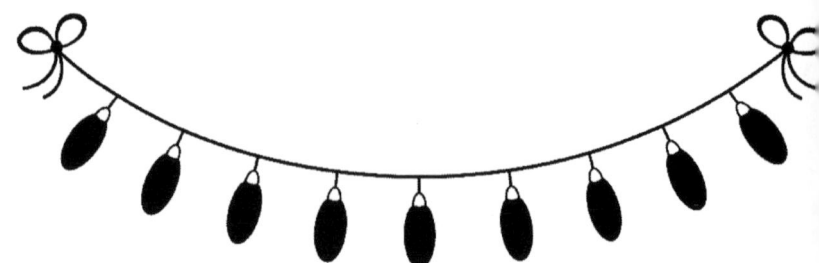

He wanted to get a little sparkle in his life!

How do you scare a snowman?

With a hair dryer.

How do men prepare their Christmas gifts?

By buying gift bags (wrapping is too complicated).

What do snowmen eat for breakfast?

Frosted flakes!

What do snowmen call their kids?

Chill-dren!

What did the snowman say to the customer?

Have an ice day!

Why did the snowman scream?

Because the snowblower was coming down the street!

What do snowmen wear on their heads?

Ice caps!

Where do snowmen keep their money?

In a snowbank!

What's a snowman's favorite greens?

Iceberg lettuce sandwiches!

Why did Santa go to music school?

He wanted to improve his wrapping skills!

What did Santa say to the smoker?

"Please don't smoke, it's bad for my ELF!"

What do you call Santa when he takes a break?

Santa Pause!

What do you call an old snowman?

Water!

Why is a Christmas tree a must for a party?

Because it always lights up the room!

What do reindeer hang on their Christmas trees?

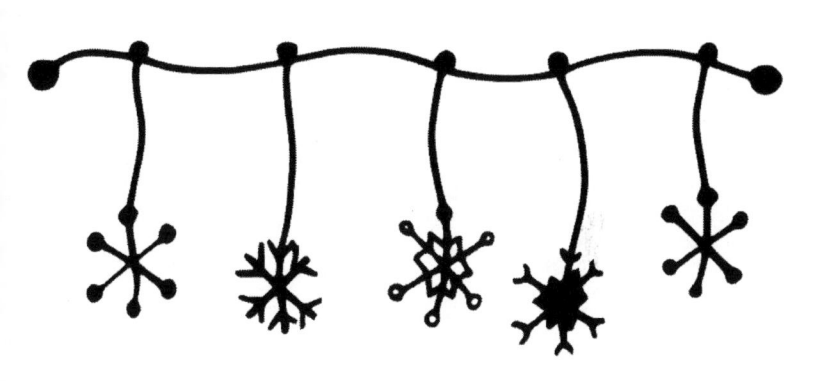

Horn-aments!

What's a reindeer's favorite game?

Stable-tennis!

KNOCK KNOCK JOKES

Hello, is anybody home? You'll want to be here for these knock-knock jokes?

Knock, knock.

Who's there?

Holly.

Holly who?

Holly-days are here again!

Knock, knock.

Who's there?

Mary.

Mary who?

Mary Christmas!

Knock, knock.
Who's there?
Snow.
Snow who?

Snow place like home for the holidays!

Knock, knock.

Who's there?

Yule.

Yule who?

Yule never guess what I got you for Christmas!

Knock, knock.

Who's there?

Donut.

Donut who?

Donut open your gifts until Christmas morning!

Knock, knock.

Who's there?

Sleigh.

Sleigh who?

Sleigh my name, sleigh my name!

Knock, knock.

Who's there?

Alpaca.

Alpaca who?

Alpaca the presents, you bring the tree!

Knock, knock.

Who's there?

Pudding.

Pudding who?

Pudding up the Christmas lights takes forever!

Knock, knock.

Who's there?

Cocoa.

Cocoa who?

Cocoa-ld outside, so let's drink some hot chocolate!

FUNNY IDEAS

Looking for something to spice up the season? Try these wild ideas to spread holiday cheer!

Candy Cane Javelin:

The goal is to throw a candy cane and make it stick upright in the snow.

Christmas Tree Limbo:

How low can you go without getting tinsel in your hair?

Gift Wrap Relay:

Race to wrap presents, but instead of tape, use spaghetti!

Twinkling Light Tag:

Turn off all the lights, and play tag with only twinkling Christmas lights to guide you.

Icicle Dueling:

Two participants, each with an icicle, try to melt the other's icicle first using just their breath.

TONGUE TWISTERS

Put that candy cane down and give your tongue a workout with these holiday themed twisters!

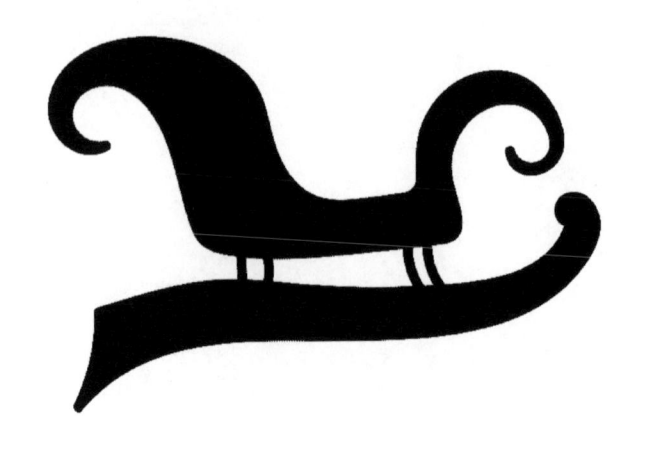

Santa's sleigh slides silently southward.

Frosty's fingers find
frozen fir trees.

Ten tiny tin trains
toot ten times.

Crisp Christmas cookies kept in crystal containers.

Sleigh bells
sing songs
so sweetly.

Gingerbread guys give great glee.

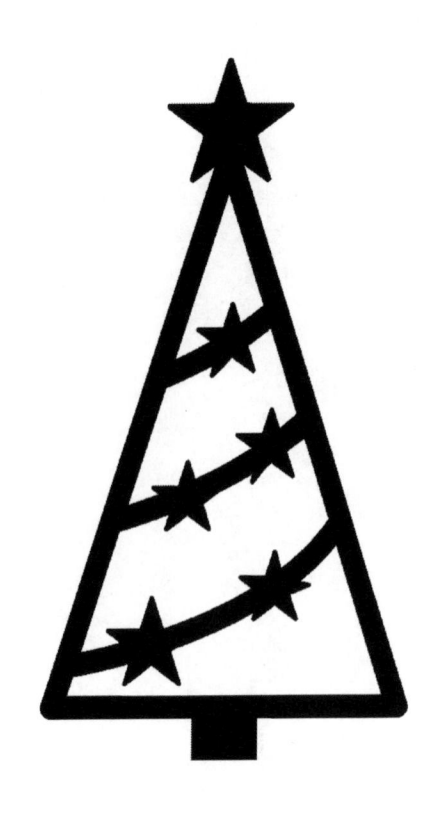

Tinsel twinkles to the top of the tree.

Five festive fairies flit freely forward.

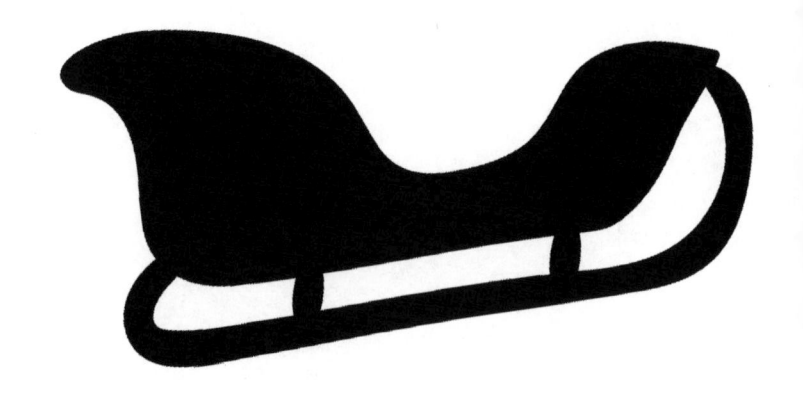

Snowflakes stick on slick sleds.

Holly hangs
heavily in
happy houses.

Elves eagerly envelope every elegant evergreen.

SILLY STORIES

What holiday faux pas have you committed? See how they stack up compared to some of these...

This Christmas, I'm giving out batteries as gifts with a note: "Toys not included."

I'm writing a book for Christmas: "How to Decorate a Tree". So far, the introduction is: "Needle-little help?"

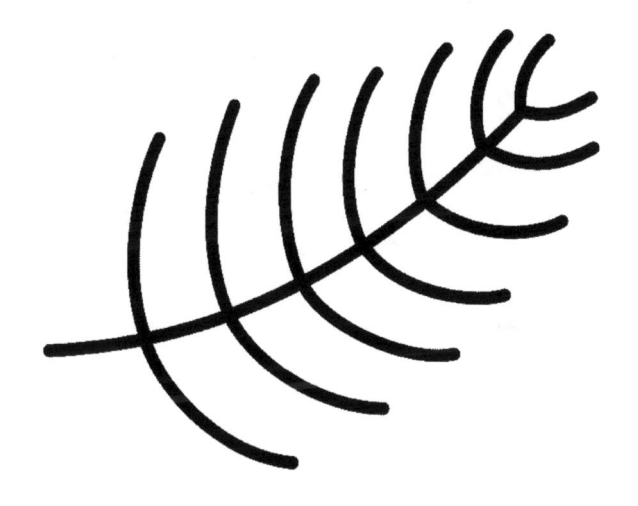

My wife asked for something sparkling for Christmas, so I got her...

A bottle of window cleaner!

My wife said she wanted something golden for Christmas, so I got her...

A goldfish!

My wife wanted
diamonds for
Christmas,
so I got her...

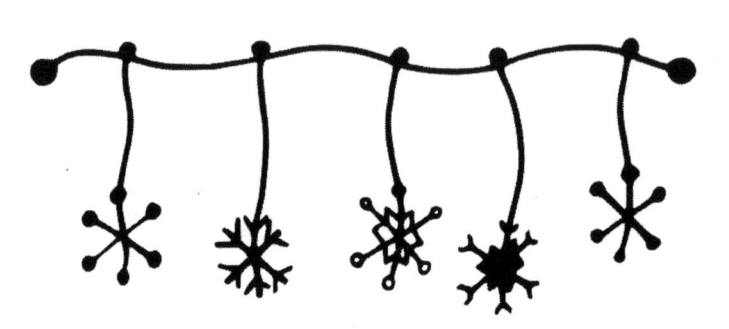

A deck of cards!

One Christmas, an elf asked a reindeer, "Do you know why Santa takes an umbrella with him on Christmas Eve?"

The reindeer replied, "No, why?"

The elf chuckled, "Because of the rain, dear!"

An elf went to a shoe store and asked for a pair of shoes, but with a twist. The shopkeeper was puzzled. "A twist?" he asked.

The elf replied, "Yes, curly toes, please. It's the latest in elf-fashion!"

RIDDLES

Get ready to stretch your brains with these puzzling riddles to chew on!

What travels around the world but always stays in one corner?

A stamp on a Christmas card.

What's as big as Santa but weighs much less?

Santa's shadow.

I have needles but can't sew. Who am I?

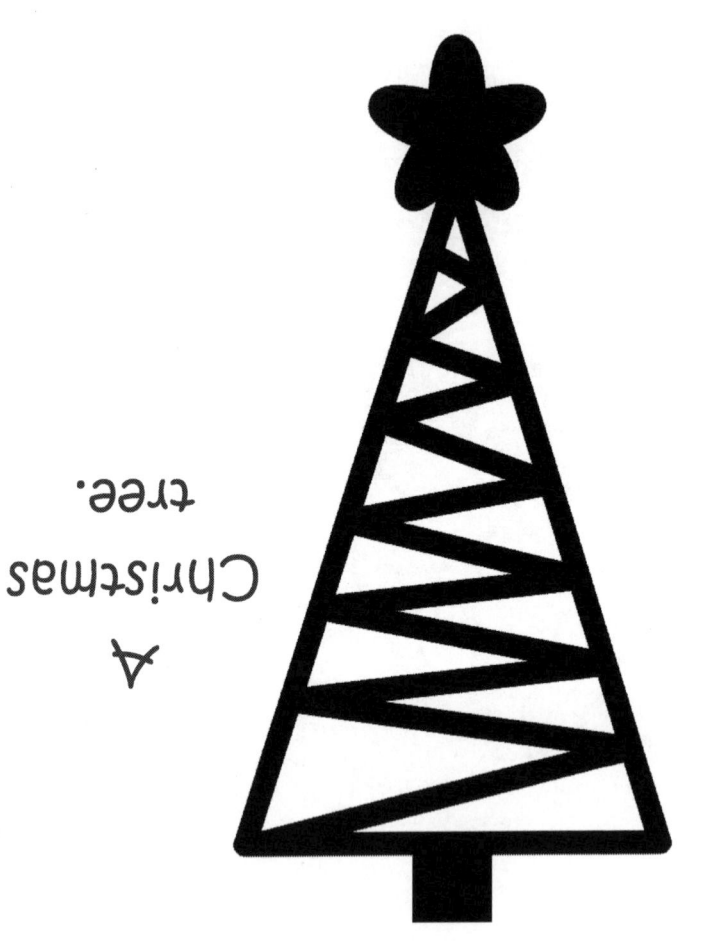

A Christmas tree.

I kiss the Earth and make it pure, yet hide the life that will endure. Who am I?

·mouS

I'm not a tree or a star overhead, but every December I'm very well-read.
Who am I?

A Christmas card.

I'm white but not a ghost, I fall but never hurt. Who am I?

Snow.

What did one plate say to another during Christmas dinner?

"Lunch is on me."

What did the Christmas tree say to the ornament?

"Quit hanging around!"

What did the big candle say to the little candle at the family Christmas gathering?

"I'm so scared of going out tonight!"

What did the stamp say to the Christmas card?

Stick with me and we'll go places!

What did one snowflake say to the other snowflake?

"You're one of a kind!"

How does Christmas
Day end?

25

¡Y a htiW

THE END

Printed in Great Britain
by Amazon